BRIGHT IDEA BOOKS

AMAZING Mountains AROUND THE WORLD

by Pat Tanumihardja

Content Consultant

Dr. Stephen Marshak
Professor of Geology
University of Illinois at Urbana-Champaign

CAPSTONE PRESS
a capstone imprint

Bright Idea Books are published by Capstone Press
1710 Roe Crest Drive, North Mankato, Minnesota 56003
www.mycapstone.com

Library of Congress Cataloging-in-Publication Data
Names: Tanumihardja, Patricia, author.
Title: Amazing mountains around the world / by Pat Tanumihardja.
Description: North Mankato, Minnesota : Capstone Press, 2019. | Series:
   Passport to nature | Includes bibliographical references and index. |
   Audience: Age 9-12. | Audience: Grade 4 to 6.
Identifiers: LCCN 2018035996 | ISBN 9781543557756 (hardcover : alk. paper) | ISBN
   9781543558074 (ebook)
Subjects: LCSH: Mountains--Juvenile literature.
Classification: LCC GB512 .T36 2019 | DDC 551.43/2--dc23
LC record available at https://lccn.loc.gov/2018035996

Editorial Credits
Editor: Claire Vanden Branden
Designer: Becky Daum
Production Specialist: Dan Peluso

Photo Credits
Alamy: Pulsar Imagens, 14–15; iStockphoto: Jef Folkerts, 5, 28, LeoPatrizi, 9, oversnap, 13, rcaucino, 6–7, Sidekick, 30–31, squashedbox, 21, Zzvet, cover; Science Source: Krafft, 23; Shutterstock Images: EastVillage Images, 24–25, Gary Saxe, 18–19, Mariusz S. Jurgielewicz, 17, Richard A McMillin, 27, Vixit, 10, 10–11

Printed in the United States of America.
PA48

TABLE OF CONTENTS

CHAPTER 1

AMAZING
Mountains

Mountains are made from rock. They take a very long time to form.

Earth is always changing. Mountains are made from Earth's surface. It is broken into huge pieces called **plates**.

Plates are always slowly moving. Sometimes one plate pushes underneath another. This lifts one side up high. This forms a mountain **range**. Other times plates run into each other. This is another way mountains are made.

Mountains can take thousands of years to form.

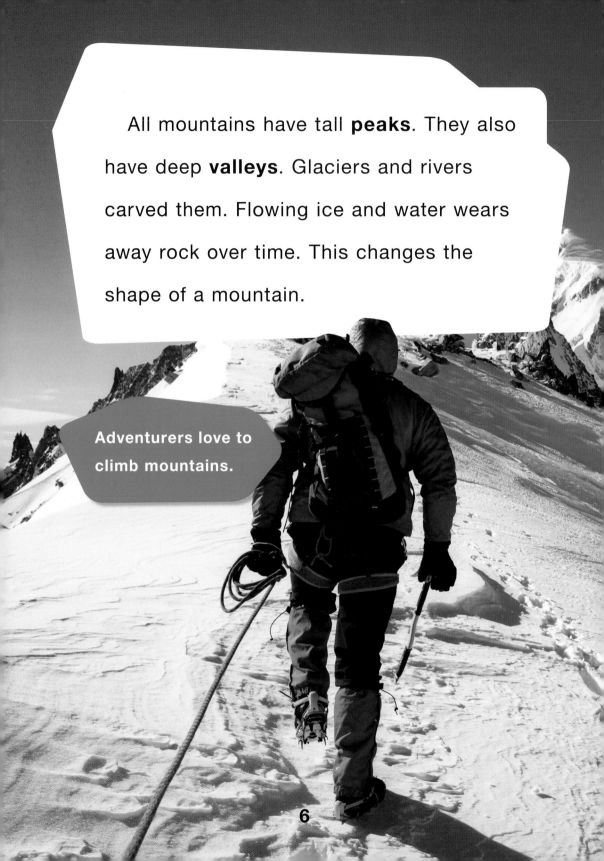

All mountains have tall **peaks**. They also have deep **valleys**. Glaciers and rivers carved them. Flowing ice and water wears away rock over time. This changes the shape of a mountain.

Adventurers love to climb mountains.

Some mountains are millions of years old. This is part of what makes them amazing. Other features make mountains amazing too. Some mountains are volcanoes. Others form underwater. Discover some of the world's most amazing mountains.

CHAPTER 2

HIMALAYAS

The Himalayas are in Asia. They are the world's tallest mountains. They have many high peaks. More than 110 are above 24,000 feet (7,315 meters). People from around the world climb these mountains.

The Himalayas began to form about 50 million years ago.

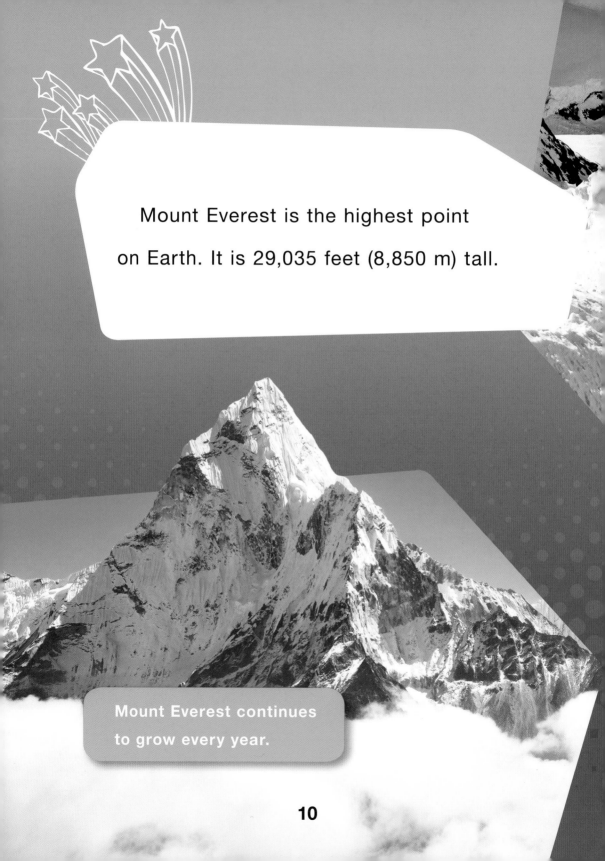

Mount Everest is the highest point on Earth. It is 29,035 feet (8,850 m) tall.

Mount Everest continues to grow every year.

Climbing Mount Everest is very hard. The full trip can take up to two months to complete.

CLIMBERS

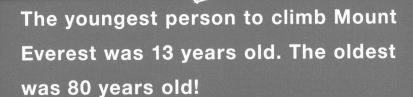

The youngest person to climb Mount Everest was 13 years old. The oldest was 80 years old!

CHAPTER 3

ANDES
Mountains

The Andes Mountains are in South America. They make up the world's longest mountain range. They are 4,500 miles (7,200 kilometers) long. They reach across seven countries.

The Andean condor
flies above the
Andes Mountains.

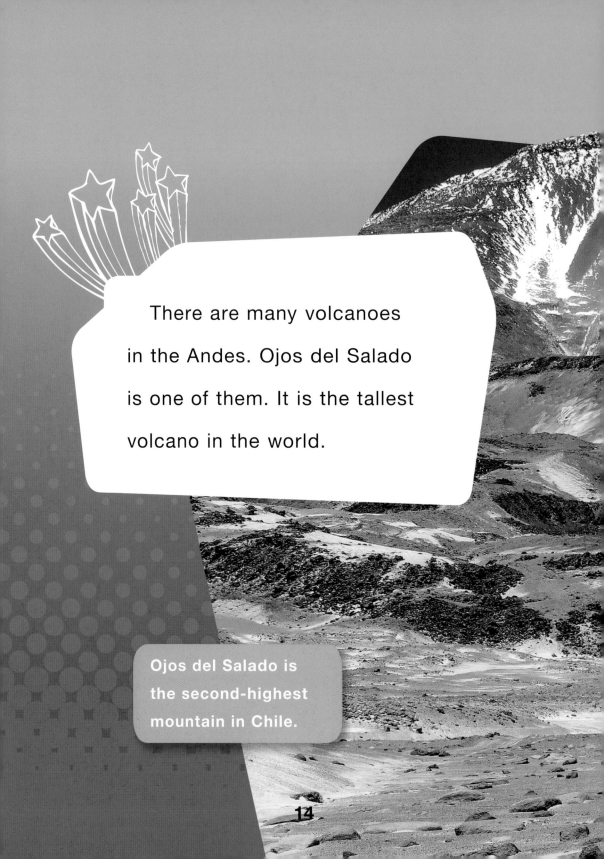

There are many volcanoes in the Andes. Ojos del Salado is one of them. It is the tallest volcano in the world.

Ojos del Salado is the second-highest mountain in Chile.

15

CHAPTER 4

SIERRA Nevada

The Sierra Nevada is a big mountain range. It runs across California and part of Nevada. Mount Whitney is its highest point. It is 14,505 feet (4,421 m) tall.

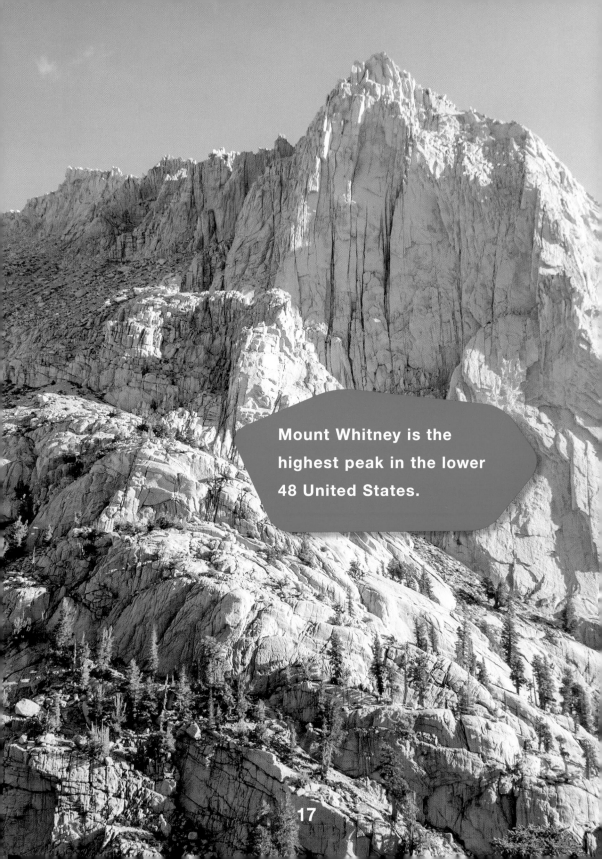

Mount Whitney is the highest peak in the lower 48 United States.

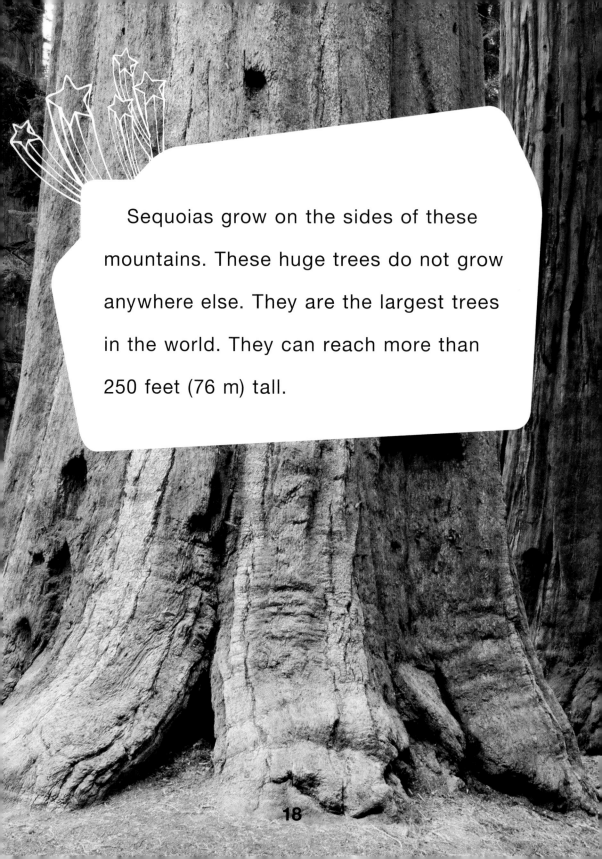

Sequoias grow on the sides of these mountains. These huge trees do not grow anywhere else. They are the largest trees in the world. They can reach more than 250 feet (76 m) tall.

Giant sequoias can be thousands of years old.

MOUNT
Kilimanjaro

Mount Kilimanjaro is the tallest volcano in Africa. It has three **volcanic cones**. Two are no longer active. One could **erupt** again someday. Nearly 25,000 people climb the mountain each year.

Elephants roam
the land below
Mount Kilimanjaro.

21

HAWAIIAN
Volcanoes

Mauna Loa is one of Earth's most active volcanoes. It is on Hawaii. It formed under the ocean long ago. Then it grew tall. Over time it grew above the water.

Hot lava flows out of Mauna Loa when it erupts.

Mauna Kea is also on Hawaii. It is the highest point on the island. More than half of it is underwater. People can go skiing here. It has snow at the top!

There are observatories on the top of Mauna Kea. Scientists study the stars there.

TALLEST MOUNTAIN

Mauna Kea is taller than Mount Everest if measured from its **base** underwater.

CHAPTER 7

MOUNT Rushmore

Mount Rushmore is in South Dakota. It is part of the Black Hills. They get their name because they look black from a distance. The highest point is Black Elk Peak. It is 7,244 feet (2,208 m) tall.

Mount Rushmore is made of a hard rock. This kind of rock is good for carving. People wanted to make faces out of the mountain. They chose four US presidents. Visitors come from around the world to see it.

The presidents on Mount Rushmore are George Washington, Thomas Jefferson, Theodore Roosevelt, and Abraham Lincoln (left to right).

GLOSSARY

base
the bottom of a mountain

erupt
when a volcano erupts, it can blow up and spit out lava, rocks, and poisonous gases

peak
the top of a mountain that comes together at a point

plate
a large piece of Earth's outer layer

range
many mountains in a row that are linked together

volcanic cone
a hill formed of rock erupted from a volcanic opening

TOP MOUNTAINS TO VISIT

ANDES MOUNTAINS, SOUTH AMERICA

Visit the longest mountain range in the world.

HIMALAYAS, ASIA

Explore the highest point on Earth.

MAUNA KEA, HAWAII

Ski down this snow-covered volcano.

MAUNA LOA, HAWAII

See one of the most active volcanoes in the world.

MOUNT KILIMANJARO, TANZANIA

Visit the highest mountain in Africa.

MOUNT RUSHMORE, SOUTH DAKOTA

Snap photos of the presidential carvings.

MOUNT WHITNEY, CALIFORNIA

See the highest peak in the lower 48 United States.

ACTIVITY

PLAN A VACATION!

Pretend you recently went on a mountain vacation. What did you pack? What did you do? What did you see? Make a scrapbook with pictures of the mountain. Cut out pictures from magazines or newspapers. Be sure to include plants, animals, and the activities you did there. Next to the pictures, write a description of what happened. At the end of the scrapbook, sum up your pretend vacation. Explain why other people should visit this mountain. Then share your scrapbook with your friends.

31

FURTHER RESOURCES

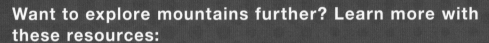

Want to explore mountains further? Learn more with these resources:

Medina, Nico. *Where Is Mount Everest?* New York: Grosset & Dunlap, 2015.

Treinish, Gregg. *Danger on the Mountain: True Stories of Extreme Adventures*. Washington, DC: National Geographic, 2016.

Ready to go out and play in the mountains? Find out what you can see and do at a mountain near you:

National Parks: Travel to National Park Mountains
https://www.nationalparks.org/connect/blog/aint-no-valley-low-enough-keep-you-getting-these-national-park-mountains

PBS Learning Media: Discover the Mountains
https://tpt.pbslearningmedia.org/resource/plum14.sci.life.discovermountains/discover-the-mountains/#.WwWamkgvw2w

INDEX